The Northern Durbar
Poems Celebrating Fifty Years of
Independence

EDITORS
Shripati Upadhyaya
Brian Lewis

Pontefract Press
IN ASSOCIATION WITH
Kala Sangam
1997

Published by **Pontefract Press**
17 Linden Terrace
Pontefract WF8 4AE, 01977-793121

Distributed by **Kala Sangam**
Carlisle Business Centre
Carlisle Road
Bradford, BD8 8BD, 01274-223212

©Text: Contributors
Cover Design: Harry Malkin
Photographs: Porl Medlock
Book Design: Brian Lewis, Reini Schühle, Harry Malkin
Printer: FM Repro, Roberttown, Liversedge
Cover Image: Deepti Desai

ISBN: 1 900325 10 1
Classification: poetry

We would especially like to thank ABL for their support of this
book in particular and for their support of Kala Sangam: The
Academy of South Asian Performing Arts.

Introduction

We came together for the fiftieth anniversary of the culmination of an independence movement; poets, dancers, photographers, lecturers, writers and, most essentially, an audience. We met in the ultra-modern hall of the Carlisle Business Centre to celebrate an event from the chronicles of a civilisation which had been in existence when the native British were food gatherers and Bradford was scrubland or forest.

The history of the land which is now the modern states of Bangladesh, India and Pakistan is a long history. What brought people together on this summer's day in 1997 was a love of that country and its relationship with the North of England. The poets who read were asked to bring poems about their feelings for the Indian subcontinent and/or their relationship with the places in which they now live.

The Northern Durbar is one of two books about the event. Poets from all the principal languages were invited to participate and contribute and quite a few of the languages of the subcontinent are represented: Kannada, Urdu, English, Hindi, Gujarati, Marathi, Tamil and Gurumukhi. It has been a challenge to publish - books with a wide variety of scripts are - and we hope that you enjoy it.

Brian Lewis and Shripati Upadhyaya

Neha Shah

Contents

Reini Schühle

*I write when I feel motivated by an
occasion or a challenge, and I love the
framework of the sonnet form. Writing
poetry is a bit like gardening. In our
small town garden, nature finds its way
out of the containment of rigid beds;
words and speech patterns break their
path through the formal structure;
although contained, they are not hemmed
in - I hope.*

Bharatha Natyam

The *Dying Swan*, organza-clouded tulle,
one leg stretched out, slim arms in resignation.
A fragile ballerina in her death throes, beautiful;
a form of art encased in rule and regulation.
The dancer, bound by code to wilfully oppose
her earthbound nature made of flesh,
tries to escape in vain through elevating pose.

In Bharatha Natyam we meet Ganesh -
feet grounded, linked to stamped and burnished soil,
the body growing from that solid contact into art.
A flow of energy, the ankle bells a counterfoil
to soles that slap, to every body part.

The dancer's grounded energy transcends;
this is where art begins and nature ends.

Mrs Ansar at the Northern Durbar

The space between the poet and the audience
assumes a quality beyond the physical dimension
for here poet and listeners are part of one experience.
'Bravo', small gestures, courteous thanks, the natural extension
of a verbal gem, with chuckles, thoughtful nods,
$\qquad\qquad\qquad\qquad\qquad$ wistful acknowledgement.
The interaction adds its weight to her recital -
the poet knows her trade, receives each compliment
with grace. The form is strong, the poet's own ghazal
takes shape secure in mutual recognition,
gives unexpected voice to what the audience express.
The contact is immediate, her intelligent rendition
is appreciated, and valued to excess.

The poet also nods, responds, adjusts her words a fraction,
the auditorium resounds with poetry in action.

Nazma Ansar

Although Nazma has a degree in Physical Education she considers that she serves literature through her hobby, writing poetry.

I will test the strength of blood

I will constantly test the strength of blood
and keep lighting the lamps even in the storm
How long will this darkness of shadows remain?

My heart, even though hurt, will be joyful
Whether I am happy or sorrowful
I will constantly recite my story.

I know that my dream world cannot become reality
but as the lightning falls I will keep smiling.
Until the climate of the garden responds
I will keep bathing in my own blood.

My tears will fall without ceasing
and the stars will shimmer.

Let this lightning waste its strength
as I keep building my home.

Although the world torments me
I will have a smile for every sorrow
and Najma will show a mirror to the enemies of love.

غزل

نجمہ خان

لہو کا ہنر آزماتے رہیں گے

چراغِ غم آندھیوں میں جلاتے رہیں گے

مسلط کہاں تک رہیں گے اندھیرے

مرے زخمِ دل مسکراتے رہیں گے

خوشی کا ہو موسم کہ غم کا ہو موسم

ہم اپنا فسانہ سناتے رہیں گے

نہ آباد ہو گی مرے دل کی دنیا

وہ برقِ تبسم گراتے رہیں گے

نہ بدلے گی جب تک فضا گلستاں کی

ہم اپنے لہو میں نہاتے رہیں گے

رہیں گے رواں میری آنکھوں سے آنسو

ستارے یونہی جھلملاتے رہیں گے

یہ برق اپنے سب حوصلے آزما لے

ہم اپنا نشیمن بناتے رہیں گے

زمانہ ستم ہم پہ ڈھاتا رہے گا

ہر اک غم پہ ہم مسکراتے رہیں گے

محبت کے دشمن ہیں جتنے بھی نجمہ

انہیں آئینہ ہم دکھاتے رہیں گے

Sathyavathi Murthy

I love performing poetry. This is also an art. A bad recitation may spoil the beauty of the poem.

Many of my poems have won prizes and have been broadcast on All India Radio. I have about seven hundred Shatpadis *to my credit which is one of the oldest styles in Kannada.*

What Is Happening To My Country?

Is this the country of Rama, Krishna and Hanuman?
Is it the resting place of truth and non violence,
the idealised land of Gandhi's dream?
Held in between Kadamba's stretched arms
I am confused by the cheating and selfishness.
There is no trace of honesty or empathy.
Sons bid for their forefather's assets;
political parties and factions mushroom everywhere
people bother about position, neglect the nation.
This "Ravana of bribe" is mightier than Ravana of Lanka.
Now it is almost like *Raktabijasura*
one evil gives birth to million others.
The general public rarely get consulted
but they are recognised only at election time
The burden of life weighs so heavy that
people cannot lift their heads
they are getting disinterested, fed up.
Politicians, you would do well to remember the legend
of the day when Bhasmasura wanted to test
Lord Shiva's boon on Shiva himself
There is but sheer aping of the western world

Where is my country leading to?

ಎತ್ತ ಸಾಗಿದೆ ನಮ್ಮನಾಡು?

ಎತ್ತ ಸಾಗಿದೆ ನಮ್ಮನಾಡು?
ರಾಮಕೃಷ್ಣರ ಬೀಡು? ವೀರ ಹನುಮನ ನಾಡು?
ಸತ್ಯ ಅಹಿಂಸೆಯ ಬೀಡು? ಗಾಂಧೀಜಿ ಯ ಕನಸಿನ ನಾಡುತ
ಕೈಗೆ ನಿಲುಕದ್ದನ್ನು ಕಬಳಿಸುವ ಕಬಂಧ ಬಾಹುಗಳು;
ಸ್ವಾರ್ಥ ಪಂಡಿತನ ವೀಣಾ ಕರಗಳ ಜಾಲಗಳು
ಪ್ರಮಾಣಿಕತೆಂದು ಗುರುತಾ ಇಲ್ಲದ ಹೂಸ್ಯ ಕಥೆಲು
ಅಪ್ಪಲ್ಪ್ಪ ಬ್ಬಿ ಹಾಕಿದ ಅಸ್ತಿಯನ್ನು ಹರಾಜು ಹಾಕುವ ಮಕ್ಕಳು;
ಬಾರ್ ಪಕ್ಕಗಳ ಗುಂಪುಗಾರಿಕೆ; ನಾಯಿಕೊಡೆಗಳು;
ರಾಷ್ಟ್ರಕ್ಕಿಂತ ಮಿಗಿಲಾದ ಕುರ್ಚಿಯ ವಿಚ್ಚಕ;
ಲಂಕಾದಿರಾವಣನ ತಲೆ ಬಾಗುವ ಲಂಕಾದಿರಾವಣನ ಅಟ್ಟಹಾಸ;
ಕಳ್ಳ ಖೀಜಾಪುರನ ಪಂಥ!
ಚಿನಾವಕೆಯ ಪ್ರಾಪ್ತಿಗೆ ಬೆಲೆ ವರಿಸಿಕೊಳ್ಳುವ ಹೆಬ್ಬನ ತಲೆಗಳು;
ತಗ್ಗಿದ ತಲೆ ವತ್ತಲುಬರದ; ವತ್ತಲೂ ಆ ಅರದ ಜನ
ನೆ ಲಾಗ ಪ್ರಾಪ್ತ್ಯ ವತ್ತು;
ಪರ ಕೊ ಬ್ರತ್ತಿ ಶಿವನ ತಲೆಂಯ ಮೇಲೇ ಕೈಯಿ ಡುವ ಭಸ್ಮಾಸುರರು;
ರಾಕ್ಷ ಬ್ರಸಾ ಟನೆ ಹೆಕಾಹುಟೀಕೆ ನುಪ ಹೊಳ್ಳವ ನಾಯಕರು;
ಪ್ರಾಪ್ತ್ಯಿಗೆ ಬಿ ಬ್ರಲ್ಲದಿದ್ದರೂ ಹುಬ್ರಗೆ ಮಲ್ಲಿಗೆ ಕ್ರಯ;
ಇವಲ್ಲದರ ನಡುವೆ ಎತ್ತ ಸಾಗಿದೆ ನಮ್ಮನಾಡು?

14

Rena Singha

Reena trained in Kathak in India with Shambu Maharaj. She has toured and performed extensively and is now settled in Canada where she has established her own company. She experiments with innovative choreography.

بریڈفورڈ شہر

دل کش ہے بریڈفورڈ کہ یہ شہر نیلا ہے
گو دور وطن سے ہے وطن ہی سی فضا ہے

آنکھوں میں محبت کے دیے سب کی ہیں روشن
چھائی یہاں ہر سمت محبت کی گھٹا ہے

دنیا کے ہر اک کونے سے یاں لوگ ہیں آباد
ہر شخص یہاں آکے بہت پھولا پھلا ہے

مسجد بھی ہے مندر بھی کلیسا بھی ہے موجود
گلشن کا ہر اک پیڑ ثمر بار ہوا ہے

ہے ربط بھی آپس کا بہت حوصلہ افزا
بے لوث عجب سلسلۂ مہر و وفا ہے

تہذیب جدا گانہ مذاہب کی ہے پھر بھی
ہر شخص یہاں زخم جدائی کی دوا ہے

یا رب ہو محبت کا چلن میرے وطن میں
نزہت کی زباں پر یہ صدا اخلاص دعا ہے

16

Nuzhat Mahmood
Nuzhat

Mrs Mahmood is a housewife who has published two poetry books. She loves music and is a keen cricket fan - especially when Pakistan wins.

City Of Bradford

The wonderful Bradford, almost a new city
although away from the homeland
it has the feel of the homeland

Everyone's eyes are lighted with feelings of love
There is always here an atmosphere of love

From every corner of the world people live here
every one has become prosperous after coming here

There are mosques, temples and also churches here
and every tree in its garden has flourished

There is so much of encouragement and amity between people
and there is abundant and continued love amidst people

Although cultures are different and so are the religions
people heal each other for the hurt of separation

Pray God ! there should be continued love in our country
Nuzhat from the bottom of her heart would just keep praying.

Malini Deshpande

Malini is based in Birmingham and devotes some of her time to raising money for a poetry group who are devoted to the memory of a young Midland poet, Gitanjali.

आगमन

कधी होईल तिचे आगमन
कांही सांगता येत नाही
हृदयाची दारं ठेवलीत उघडी
पापण्यांची झालरही त्यावर लावली

पण ती कधी येईल अचानक
सांगता येत नाही
देव कधी प्रसन्न होईल
भक्त सांगू शकत नाही

पाउस कधी कोसलेल
आपल्या हाती नाही
पाहुणे येतील कधी अचानक
कांही सांगता येत नाही

म्हणूनच जगण्याचा प्रयत्न
करते मी सदा
कारण झोपी राहून
चालणार नाही मला

कारण तीचे आगमन
फार सुखावह आहे
वाटते ईश्वराचा घरून
निरोप घेरून आली आहे

देवाच्या जणु घरूनच ती येते
सुंदर पदन्यास घालत
हृदय मंचकावर नृत्य करते
मन होते धूंद नशेने हलके होते

सुंदर अर्थमधूर शब्दांच्या
तारा झणकारतात
सरस्वतीच्या वीणेची
नादमय वळये उठलात

देउन सार संपल्यावर
मेघ जसे रीक्त होतात
तप्त करून धरतीला
आनंद तीचा अनुभवतात

तसेच ती आल्यावर
ओझे उतरते मनावरचे
नवनिर्मितीचा होतो आनंद
स्रजन शीलतेलाही सुटतो गंध

मूल कसेही असो
वाटे मातेला प्रियेचा
म्हणूनच जोपासनाही होते
त्याचीही हृदयाच्या तुकडयाप्रमाणे अलगदच!!

Arrival

No one can tell when the thoughts arrive,
Just keep your heart and eyes open
Still you can't tell when she will appear
Just like a devotee is unable to predict
the moment of God's blessing
Forecasting rain is unpredictable
So is the arrival of uninvited guest
That's why I keep try stay awake
The thought, the inspiration, the experience is so thrilling
It comes like message from God
The graceful thoughts that come dancing
make my mind intoxicated
The beautiful meaningful words
are like sounds from Saraswati's Veena
The cloudburst quenches the thirst of mother earth
Once the inspiration takes the concrete form
the joy of creation is very enchanting
Like a child is beautiful to his mother
no matter what the world thinks
It will be my creation, a piece of my heart.

Ismail B Patel (Babar)

Ismail B Patel (Babar) is a Lancashire teacher. He has published collections of poems and is the chairman of the Gujarati Writers Association.

પરદેશમાં

કોઈ ના ભૂલે કદી તારું જતન પરદેશમાં
યાદ આવે છે મને મારું વતન પરદેશમાં

એટલે તારી છબીને ઉપર ટાંગી દીધી
કે મને મળશે નહી તારું વદન પરદેશમાં

પ્રેમપત્રો વાંચીને અશ્રુઓ આંખોથી વહે,
ના હવે દેખી શકીશ તારા નયન પરદેશમાં

એમ તો છે દૂર મારાથી વસ્યાં એ તે છતાં
મને કહે છે કોક 'દિ થાશે મિલન પરદેશમાં

ખેલ છે કિસ્મત તણો એ માં સનમ તું શું કરે?
કેટલા કિસ્સા છે અહિયાં ગુલવદન પરદેશમાં

ચંદ્રમા તો ડાઘ છે પણ તું પ્રિયે બેદાગ છે,
દિલ મહી ઓ દિલરુબા તારું સદન પરદેશમાં

તાજ સમ કોઈ ઈમારત ના મળે દુનિયા મહી,
ના મળે અહિયાં વળી એવાં ભવન પરદેશમાં

કઈ રીતે 'બાબર' તને ભૂલે કે એને રાત દિ'
યાદ આવે હરઘડી તારા કથન પરદેશમાં

Abroad (in the foreign land)

No body should forget their culture in the foreign land.
I miss my home country while living in the foreign land.
That's why I have placed your image in my heart;
for I will not be able to keep your promises in the foreign land.
As I read your love letters, my tears flow
for I cannot see your eyes in this foreign land.
As such we are distance apart
some one says we will meet one day abroad.
This is the play of fate, what can I do my love
there are several stories of people falling in love here.
The moon has shadow but dear you are without blemish.
You will always reside in my heart in this foreign land,
There is no monument like Taj Mahal in this world.
You can not see a building like that in this foreign land.
Babar says, "I tried to forget you in several ways"
but I remember your words every moment in this foreign world.

Geetha Upadhyaya

*Geetha is the Artistic Director of Kala
Sangam, the South Asian Academy of
Performing Arts and its principal Bharat
Natyam dancer.*

The Durbar In The North

Tamil everywhere
in everything there was Tamil
in those days.

Tamil everywhere
Tamil in everything - it was those days.

Now where and whence is Tamil?
I searched till my eyes grew tired
Wandered till my feet grew weary
Thirsting for Tamil.

Softly like the southern breeze she touched - Mother Tamil
Embracing me with gentle hands.

The Lord of the one who dwells in the Lotus
Has been united with the snow headed one and
the group who are ABL

Arise - here is the Northern Durbar

Revived I was in Urdu
In Gujrati I toddled
Overjoyed I was in Hindi
Marathi made my hair stand on end
Chivalry flowed in Kannada
Rejoice I did in English.
But I saluted in Tamil.

Make your blessings flow, Mother Tamil
May these poets grow
To create such Durbars
as long as these languages live
Long live the mother tongue
Long live Tamil!

தர்பாரில் தமிழ் தாய்

எங்கும் தமிழ் எதிலும் தமிழ் – அன்று

எங்கும் தமிழ் எதிலும் தமிழ் – ஆனால் இன்றோ

எங்கே தமிழ் எதோ தமிழ் ?

தேடினேன் விழி சோர்ந்தேன்

அலைந்தேன் தாள் துவண்டேன்

தவித்தேன் தமிழ் தாகத்தால்

தீண்டினாள் தென்றலாய் தாய் – தமிழ் தாய்

அணைத்தாள் மென்கரத்தால் – தமிழ் கரத்தால்

இணைத்தாள் கமலையின் நாயகனே அப்பனித்தலையனுடன்

சேர்த்தாள் எ.பி.ல். கூட்டத்துடன்

உருவாக்கிதந்தாள் இவ்வின்பகவியரங்கம்

உயிர்மெழுந்தேன் உருதுவில்

குலாவினேன் குஜராத்தியில்

இன்பமுற்றேன் இந்தியில்

மெய்சிலிர்த்தேன் மராட்டியில்

வீரமுற்றேன் வங்கத்தில்

களித்தேன் கன்னடத்தில்

ஆனந்தித்தேன் ஆங்கிலத்தில்

தூலவணங்கினேன் தமிழில்

வேண்டினேன் தமிழ் தாயிடம்

நல்லாசி பொழிந்தருள் – கவிகூட்டத்தின்மேல்

நல்வாக்கு தந்தருள் – கவியரங்கங்கள் வளர

வாழிய தாய் மொழி

வாழிய செந்தமிழ் !

Kala Sangam was founded in 1993 by the Bharat Natyam dancer Dr Geetha Upadhyaya and her husband Dr Shripati Upadhyaya, an enthusiast of Indian languages and literature. The company is now well established in Bradford, Leeds, Ashton, Bolton, Hull, Newcastle and Manchester. It offers classes in dance, tabla and the cultures of the Indian subcontinent. Musicians and dancers regularly give recitals on its behalf.

Jeanne Ellin

My poems were written as a tribute to that unknown Asian woman five generations back in my family's history, the Dark Mother of my line.

Like many 'Anglo-Indians' my family denied and derided the Indian part of our heritage. I feel keenly the loss of half my potential heritage, and great sadness.

A Gift For Grandmother
Since I cannot know

Since I cannot know how you came together
Nor what it was you felt towards that man
Of another race and tongue, his mind formed
And fed on conqueror's meat, I can only

Speculate, count the possibilities like
Prune stones round a plate. Coercion,
Commerce, compliance, need, greed or
Perhaps just a price agreed. Yet still

I will hope your bodies bridged with
Gentle touch and stranger's smiles, I
will hope your minds reached beyond
Alien skin and found a wordless core

Of trust, even though its grace lasted
Only until your bodies peeled apart.

Grandmother

You brought a heritage of songs and dreams, but they were
Left to decay within your open palms, as your children turned
Their faces from your dark gaze, and stopped their ears to your
Stories, longing only for their father's powerful pallor.

They let your name decay unused, smothered you with silence
Ignored your presence and denied the very rumour of your
Life. So impoverished, I can not search out your home, learn
Your stories not hear your songs, or honour your faith.

Leaving me the only gift of yours that denial could not
Quench. These rich tints of hair and skin that link me
Irrevocably to you. Mark me yours beyond dispute, Dark
Mother I walk in your skin. Your granddaughter at last.

Deepti Desai

Eileen Wright

The following poems, selected from my poem sequence, Migration, *reflect on Anglo-Indian experiences. 'They Were Ready' describes the long-term effects of mixed identity, colonialisation, and migration. Losing culture, Anglo-Indians belonged nowhere, not even when 'returning' at Partition to England, which was (so unrealistically) dreamt of as 'Home'.*

36

Voices

i am a child in time
who's lost the voices of the past
familiar sounds i took for granted
thought would last
anti-European rise and fall
of my grandmother
as she gossiped
over endless cups of hot sweet tea
rising rising rising
and falling
over me
and the people
she brought with her
with names like Smiler
Duchess and Slim
the man who always wore
dark glasses
never spoke to me
looking from
his one brown one blue eye
East and West met
in him uneasily
while i sat listening
child in the corner
while they flowed on
voices echoing in each other
rising rising rising
and falling
over me.

They Were Ready

They were ready for the journey Home
talk would come around to this
'the place we left behind'
but Home was invention, glorified dream
no one was waiting there
They were ready
for their second migration
Out of India this time
first they'd left Ireland
hoping for new lives
leaving everything behind
And they were ready
but 1947 was a shock
dream became uneasy reality
suddenly saying goodbye
to several hundred years
though they were seen
by everyone as interlopers now
perhaps they'd always been
They were ready
but two centuries
of travelling wearies the soul
all they knew was how to take risks
to move into a new place
as if they owned it

Shripati Upadhyaya

Susan's story is from a series about people with mental handicap. In India such people mostly live with their families. Here it is different as most of the people with mental handicap live in and are cared for in group homes.

Here are the glimpses of people living in the group homes who are seemingly fighting harder for their identity saying, 'Look, I am alive, not dead.'

Susan's Story Lacked Words

I know your name is Susan but who are you?
You do not have the words
You are unknown
Those who surround you also lack direction, are lost
but claim to understand your identity
In such a crowd - how lonely
Susan's eyes are red
She breathes deeply, she is aware of her life
She has pulled somebody's hair
and bitten someone else,
people move around her trying to control her
They are upset, ask "Susan do you do this to mock us ?
Somebody says "Deny her food
Do that and she will come to her senses"
Susan eyes are red.
She breathes deeply
Her thoughts are elsewhere, she's lost
Is this life or is it a joke
"Neither home nor relatives
Nobody has visited for several Christmases
But many seem to own me".
They say "stop misbehaving only then
Will somebody come to see you"
Susan's eyes are red.
She breathes deeply,
More thoughts surface

She is aware of her own life
There are still strengths in life
She has scratched somebody
Thrown somebody's dinner
There is chaos
In the T.V. room Susan is alone.
people are whispering "Nobody can see the telly now"
Susan's eyes are red.
She breathes deeply,
Susan has become quiet
She has pushed away her dinner.
People say "You have started another drama
If you don't eat, don't eat"
Susan's eyes are blank
People realised that Susan is changing
Where is the temper, where is the strength ?
The G.P comes, confirms a tumor
They say she is ill
She will be a guest for but a few days
I know your name is Susan but who are you ?
You do not have the words
You are unknown
Those who surround you also lack direction, are lost
but claim to understand your identity
In such a crowd - how lonely.

सूसन की कहानी बेजबानी

जानता हूँ तुम्हारा नाम सूसन है
पर किसकी पहचान हो तुम ?
तुम्हारे पास तो अल्फाज नहीं है
कितने अनजान हो तुम
तुम्हारे इर्द गिर्द भटकते से लोग
इस भरी भीड में कितने वीरान हो तु.म

सूसन की ऑंखें लाल हैं
गहरी सासों के बीच
उसे अपनी
जिन्दगी का अहसास है
उसने किसी के बाल खीचें है
तो किसी को काट खाया है

इर्द गिर्द घूमते हुए लोग
अपनी ताकत की आजमाइशी
करते हुए लोग
परेशान हैं
उन्हें चिढाने के लिए
कर रही है सूसन
यह सब कुछ

कोई कहता है बॉधा दो उसके हाथा
किसी ने कहा खाना न देना
ठिकाने आ जायेगी अपने आप

गहरी सॉसों के बीच
सूसन की ऑंखें लाल हैं
कहीं और हैं खयाल उसके
यह मजाक है या जिन्दगी
न घर न रिश्तेदार
कोई मिलने भी नहीं आया
पिछले 12 क्रिसमस से
फिर भी इतने सारे दावेदार
जो कहते हैं
बद करो ये शरारत
तभी मिलने आयेगा तुमसे कोई

सूसन की आँखें लाल हैं
गहरी साँसों के बीच
और कॉफी खयाल उभरें हैं
उसे अपनी जिन्दगी का अहसास है
जिन्दगी के तबके अभी बाकी हैं
उसने किसी को खरोंचा है
किसी के खाने की थाली फेंक दी है

तहलका मच गया है
टी वी के कमरे में सिर्फ सूसन है
नहीं अब कोई टी वी नहीं देख पायेगा
दबी जबानों में कहते हुए लोग

सूसन की आँखें लाल हैं
गहरी साँसों के बीच
उसने चुप्पी साध ली है
ठेल दी है उसने खाने की थाली
लोग कहते हैं
सूसन ने दूसरा तमाशा शुरु किया है
न खाये तो मत खाये

सूसन की आँखें सूनी है
लोगो को अहसास हुआ है
कि सूसन बदल रही है
कहाँ है वह तेजी कहाँ है वह जोश
कल जी पी आया था
एक्सरे की बात हुई है
सूसन को टयुमर है
कहते हैं सूसन बीमार है
थोडे दिनों की मेहमान है

जानता हूँ तुम्हारा नाम सूसन है
पर किसकी पहचान हो तुम ?
तुम्हारे पास तो अल्फाज नहीं है
कितने अनजान हो तुम
तुम्हारे इर्द गिर्द भटकते से लोग
इस भरी भीड में कितने वीरान हो तुम

Brian Lewis

*These two Shiva poems are from a very
long narrative poem called* The Galleries
Of Leed*s. The central character, an
unemployed young woman, Jude, has
been touring Hell with Virgil looking at
sculpture. Suddenly she glances Heaven
and sees a statue of a Hindu god.*

Two Siva Poems

High on a hill, catching the day's last light, a bronze of the great
lord, Lord Siva; the Hindu God whose dance we call Creation.
Jude heard a little drum, felt the wind brush on her cheek; hate
left her as she stood stock still below, staring in fascination.
'He seems to move,' she said, 'but gloaming can play tricks;
has he four arms and each one different?'

Virgil - 'Men are sticks
that break but such as he will never break, in rhythm turning,
reaching perfect pitch, he is the energy that lets us cope
and as the world revolves he watches as we wake each morning,
sees us don our clothes and seek for stardust. He's Hope
as energy drawn as a symbol which plays out the universal fight
of Good and Evil. He stamps on Ignorance, puts an end to night.

'But still night draws us in,' said Jude and shuddered, 'soon
it will be dark.'

       'But look, he's ribbons in his hair; the Plough,
Orian, Dorado, Libra, all there and on his head the Moon.'

'That will reflect his glory through the night. And now
I look more closely, at the crown of that Lord's tangled hair,
a human skull.'
       'We're dancing always to the Dance of Death,
and that's for sure,' Jude said and sighed.
                       Virgil - 'I fear
nothing is for certain.' He glanced away. 'My next breath
may be my last and if it is who'll render all these broken lines
to sense? No one. I am unique, my logic's all my own, yet
for all that I dance with Siva. With death Empire falls, declines
to rubble and yet the dance goes on. In dancing I come to get
the energy to render and return. There's no rewards. I am, I act,
because I know I dance up to my limits; and that's a fact.'

Krishna Kumar Mittal

Krishna Kumar Mittal is a retired lecturer in Modern Arts and Languages active in the Bradford Indian Cultural Organisations. He writes in Panjabi, Hindi and Urdu.

In Your Love

In your love I spent my entire life
Pray God! allow me in your Kingdom

I am caught in a deadly storm;
I have lost my darling to this world

It is your grace, that, I am in your vision;
otherwise my soul, would have been your care.

I am entrapped and caught in the false glory

I will see her, in God's Kingdom
For ages "Mittal", I have longed for this.

ਲਲਕਨਾ

ਗੁਜ਼ਾਰਿਯਾ ਯੇ ਸਾਰਾ ਜ਼ੀਵਨ ਤੇਰੇ ਪਿਯਾਰ ਵਿਚ
ਰਬਬਾ ਹੁਣ ਬੁਲਾਓ ਮੈਨੂੰ ਆਪਣੇ ਦਿਯਾਰ ਵਿਚ
ਹੁਣ ਮੈਂ ਹਾਂ, ਅਤੇ ਹੈ ਮੌਤ ਦੀ ਤੇਜ਼ ਹਨੇਰੀ
ਪੀਰਤਮ ਮੇਰਾ ਹੋਯਾ ਯੇ ਗੁਮ, ਇਸ ਸੰਸਾਰ ਵਿਚ

ਹੈ ਤੇਰਾ ਕਰਸ ਕਿ ਮੈਂ ਹਾਂ ਤੇਰੀ ਨਜ਼ਰ ਵਿਚ
ਨਹੀਂ ਤਾਂ ਹੋਵੇ ਮੇਰੀ ਯੇ ਜ਼ਾਤ ਤੇਰੀ ਫ਼ਿਕਰ ਵਿਚ

ਹੈ ਮੇਰੇ ਆਲੇ ਦੁਵਾਲੇ ਮੇਰੀ ਜ਼ਾਤ ਦੀ ਦਿਵਾਰ
ਫਸ ਗਯਾ ਹਾਂ ਮੈਂ ਝੂਟੀ ਸ਼ਾਨ ਵਿਚ
ਦਰਸ਼ਨ ਹੋਂਣ ਮੈਨੂੰ ਓਸਦੇ, ਰਬ ਦੇ ਦਯਾਰ ਵਿਚ
ਕਿਨੇ ਚਿਰ ਤੋਂ ਹੈ ਕਿਸ਼ਨ ਮਿਤਤਲ ਇਸਹੇ ਇੰਤਜ਼ਾਰ ਵਿਚ

Kala Sangam is a secular organisation which works across cultures. Since its title means the merging of the arts it works regularly with poets, writers, performers, actors, musicians, and, as here, with publishers.

It is especially committed to using South Asian Performing Arts with people with disability and to this end has evolved a project called Sacar.

Its headquartes are located in the Carlisle Business Centre, Carlisle Road, Bradford.

Uma Parameswaran

Uma Parameswaran is the Professor of English Literature at Winnipeg University.

Amma, I Like School

Amma, I like school,
It is such fun,
We play most of the time
And sing songs in French.
Amma, finger-painting is such fun
So many bright bright colours
And we can use all we want.
Amma, if a crayon breaks
You can just throw it away
And take a new one!
Ma, you think you could change my name
To Jim or David or something?
Amma, I love recess time.
Did you see the tyres?
The tyres tied together?
I can climb up
And sit inside and swing
Such fun.
When winter comes
I'll turn less brown
Won't I, ma?
It would be nice to be
Like everyone else, you know?

Under A Sky

Under a sky more vast than any I've seen.
On snow more cold that ever I dreamed,
I stand alone
Amid masks that speak an alien tongue.
Far far are those I loved and love
And far the fragrance of my native flowers
O'er which bees murmur homeland tunes.

Small comfort I find in these needle pines
That stand bleak against the white.
Where's the fire that can sustain us
In this alien land of endless skies?
Where the friend who'll lend a hand
So we stand tall in our own eyes?

Under a sky bluer than any I've seen
On snow whiter than ever I dreamed
I stand beside the Golden Boy
Holding golden sheafs of corn
Against a dawn heralding the joy
Of years to come.

Zohra Jabeen

*Zohra is a maths and science teacher in
Bradford middle school. She has written
three books for children.*

*The following poem was translated into
English by Mohammed Jamal.*

عید کی شام

کس قدر اداس ہے عید کی شام
تا حد نظر دُھند
کہر، بارش، دھواں
خامشی بیکراں
کبھی یہ موسم بہامی ہوا کرتا تھا
اُمنگوں کا
چاہتوں کا
لے نکلتا انجانی منزلوں کی اور
ان جلی راہوں پر
اچھوتے جذبوں سے
ان کے خوابوں کی طرف

. . . .

اب یہ سنبھل ہے اداسی کا
خانہ دل ویران و سنسان
کپکپی سی در آئی ہے
جسم و جان میں
آج ملن کے دن بھی
ہر سُو تکلف
ہر طرف بیگانگی کے سائے ہیں
نہ غم نہ خوشی
نہ درد آشنا چہرہ
دل حزیں ترس گیا ہے
خوش رنگ نظاروں،
نظر نواز لوگوں کو

. . . .

بھرے گھرانوں میں ہنگامہ عید
خاطریں، دعوتیں، ملاقاتیں
چہچے، قہقہے، شوخیاں
سر سراتے آنچلوں کی اوٹ میں
فوارے ہنسی کے
پھر رات گئے

سخت پردہ میں محفلیں بزرگوں کی
ــ ــ ــ
امی
یہ عید ہے
آپ کے بچپن کی عیدوں جیسی
نہیں میری جان!
میں باہوں میں سمیٹ لیتی ہوں اپنے جگر پاروں کو

Eid Evening

How sad this evening is enveloped in mist
rain, smoke, endless silence.
There was a time when this season beckoned us
full of yearnings, hopes and longing
towards new destinations, uncharted routes;
away from petty desire towards enchanted dreams.

Now it is a symbol of sorrow,
the abode of the heart; a wilderness
a shiver descends on the body and soul .
Even on this day of greetings
everywhere there is hesitancy and indifference,
neither happiness nor pain nor a sensitive face.
My heavy heart yearns for the colourful sights
of generous people.

In houses full of people
the commotion of celebration -
parties, meetings, entertaining laughter, giggles, smiles
hidden in veils and scarves - fountains of laughter.
Then late at night
the gathering of venerable elders.

This is a mother's Eid,
not the one you loved in childhood, my dear.
I bend and gather up my loved ones
in my arms.

Julie Cockburn

Julie Cockburn was born in England of parents from Lahore and she was raised on stories from the subcontinent. She feels that it is important to communicate that part of her life in her poetry.

Me and the G-nome

A tiny atom of being linked to the ancestors.
Random cells flung together at conception,
Carrying messages through the generations.
My nose grew along family lines.
Big toes curved up,
Long brown fingers.
Images and patterns printed there
as the cells grew and divided.
My history in the wrinkles on my palms.

Family Tree

Lost Generations,
Unsatisfied ghosts,
Silent women calling me -
for recognition,
for vengeance,
for a Name.
Breeders on the male line.
Culture suffocated,
Genius lost,
Artist unknown,
Nobody.

Mini Mushaira

*Mini Mushaira is a group of three
professional Northern poets, Nasir
Sultan Kazmi, Debjani Chatterji and
Simon Fletcher.*

So much to say *was translated into
English by the author Nasir Kazmi and
Debjani Chatterjee.*

A prayer for the well-being of Nasir Kazmi's House

"The man who plants trees does
not always live to enjoy the fruit."

Let white doves continue to crowd
the roof of Nasir Kazmi's house.

May the kites, saffron, peacock-blue,
play above Nasir Kazmi's house.

Let crimson roses, bushes, trees,
thrive around Nasir Kazmi's house.

May the sun shine, rains in season
fall down on Nasir Kazmi's house.

Let the family, gentle, learned,
live long in Nasir Kazmi's house.

Simon Fletcher

خط میں کیا کیا لکھوں یاد آتی ہے ہر بات پہ بات
یہی بہتر کہ اُٹھا رکھوں ملاقات پہ بات

رات کو کہتے ہیں کل بات کریں گے دن میں
دن گذر جائے تو سمجھو کہ گئی رات پہ بات

اپنی باتوں کے زمانے تو ہوا بُرد ہوئے
اب کیا کرتے ہیں ہم صورتِ حالات پہ بات

لوگ جب ملتے ہیں کہتے ہیں کوئی بات کرو
جیسے رکھی ہوتی ہوتی ہو مرے ہات پہ بات

مِل نہ سکنے کے بہانے اُنہیں آتے ہیں بہت
ڈھونڈ لیتے ہیں کوئی ہم بھی ملاقات پہ بات

دوسروں کو بھی مزا سننے میں آتے باہر
اپنے آنسو کی نہیں کیجیے برسات پہ بات
۱۹۹۲ء

So Much To Say

So much comes to mind for writing in my letter
That it's better saved for when we finally meet.

At night we say: "Let's talk tomorrow, in daylight."
But as the day passes, we'll say: "Let's talk at night."

Our intimate talks are blown away with the past.
These days all we hear is talk of current affairs.

Whenever I meet people they ask: "Say something,"
As though I always have some ready speech to hand.

My friend knows many excuses for not meeting.
I too find some reason or other when paths cross.

So that others may take pleasure in your talk, Basir,
Don't speak of your tears, talk rather about the rain.

Basir Sultan Kazmi

Dancing Ganapati

Dancing Ganapati, trunk in the air,
we loved you and fed you on milk and sweets,
smeared sandal paste on your marble brow,
decked your pachyderm neck with fresh marigold,
beat on our drums and danced, while you stared
with ears fanned out as we hailed you with joy.
We waved oil lamps and swayed as we sang;
"Dancing Ganapati, trunk in the air,
bless us who worship with milk and sweets."

We slipped away, ate and drank in your name,
Life was as always, stone-fleshed together,
you were our friend, we knew where we stood.
Dancing Ganapati, trunk in the air,
we drank your milk and savoured your sweets
till the day you chose to take our treats -
we wondered where all the milk had gone,
and stared in disbelief at our old playmate;
dancing Ganapati, trunk in the milk!

Debjani Chatterjee